OVERCOMER

A Memoir

MARIA DRAKE

Publisher: *MCOLLINSENTERPRISES*

Book Coach, Interior Layout, and Art Director: *Michelle Collins*

Dedication

I dedicate this book to my beautiful daughter. I not only love you but I really like you, adore you, and treasure you. We went through so many struggles together but we had each other to rely on. You have been my reason to be strong, to overcome life's hurdles in my path, and to remain strong in my faith, trusting in God no matter what. I thank God for His hand upon you as well. You have turned out to be an incredible, amazing daughter. Your determination has taken you far in life. You have accomplished so much more than ever expected. Thank you for telling me that I was your inspiration!

I also want to dedicate this book to all the women who feel abandoned and/or forsaken by God. Life is not fair, but God never said that life was fair. We all have trials and tribulations. We all at one time or another have been abused, rejected, experienced a loss of a loved one, financial difficulties, wondering how am I going to pay for this or that, loneliness, sickness, being violated, hurt, slandered against, and broken. I know how you feel. I was there, however my faithfulness in God never ceased even though there were many times I felt so alone in this world and my prayers were falling on deaf ears.

I pray that as you read my life story, it will give you hope and increase your faith in God to trust Him. I leave you with this scripture in John 16:33 (NIV) *"I have told you these things, so that in me you may have peace. In this world you will have trouble. But take heart! I have OVERCOME the world."*

A Memoir...

Table of Contents

Acknowledgments

First, I thank God and give him all the GLORY for being with me from the beginning of time and leading me into wholeness. If it was not for God in my life, I would not be here at all.

I want to thank my husband, Frank Agosto, whom I love very much for being so supportive and encouraging me. From the very beginning when I shared with him of wanting to write a book on my life, he has been there for me as I tackled this endeavor.

To my beautiful daughter, Patricia Drake, for making me a VERY proud parent. You gave me the motivation not to give up. You are my hero.

I want to personally acknowledge someone who is very dear to me, someone whom I love, respect, admire, and consider her as my spiritual leader, Dr. Pastor Keisha Lewis. Dr. Keisha and her husband Dr. Russell Lewis are the Founders and Senior Pastors of Ultimate Life Church. Dr. Keisha is also the Founder of Keisha Lewis Ministries, a prayer life line ministering to women. She has such a big heart and passion for issues and challenges that face women today. Thank you for your prayers, encouragement, and support you have given me.

Thank you to the beautiful talented Pastor/Coach Michelle Collins, for your coaching, guidance, and encouragement as the book was being developed. I thank God for the divine connection. I appreciate you and enjoyed working with you. Not only were you my Coach, but also my Publisher! God sent me a bundle package, all-in-one!

Special thanks to those who endorsed my Book, Bishop Dr. Eric O. Minta, Pastor Patricia Muiruri, and Minister Veda Platt

Foreword

The importance of understanding and embracing our journey, are essential elements to fulfilling our life's purpose. Today, considering the times we currently live in, it is very important to identify with our journey and ensure that our journey serves its purpose to fuel our future.

Time and time again in the bible we see how God uses the journey of people to prepare them for the purpose he had planned in their future. The bible teaches us in Romans 8:28, *"That we know all things work together for good to those who love God, to those who are the called according to His purpose."* God ensures us through scripture that our journey, in spite of the ups and downs, highs and lows, will ultimately work together for our good and bring us into God's purpose for our lives.

Life is a journey filled with lessons, hardships, heartaches, joys, celebrations, and special moments that will ultimately lead us to our destination, of purpose in life. The road will not always be smooth. In fact, throughout our travels, we will encounter many challenges. Some of these challenges will test our courage, strengths, weaknesses, and faith.

As you read this book, you will discover through Maria Drake's journey that God is always in control even when it doesn't look like it and all He requires of us is to trust in Him and the process of life. As God was with this incredible woman throughout her journey, let it be a testament to His faithfulness in the lives of His children!

~ **Dr. Keisha Lewis**

Co-Pastor Ultimate Life Church, CEO Keisha Lewis, Ministries

Introduction

Do you remember the movie "Forrest Gump?" It came out in 1994 and Forrest Gump was the lead character played by Tom Hanks. The famous line that caught everybody's attention was *"My mom always said life was like a box of chocolates. You never know what you're gonna get."* I love this metaphor for life. The chocolates in the box come in various shapes, sizes, and flavors. Each time you take a chocolate, you have no idea what flavor it's inside until you bite into it. Life is so much like that, full of surprises!

Regardless of where you find yourself about the choices you have made, as a follower and believer of Christ, we can be overcomers if we successfully resist the power and temptation of the world's system by remaining steadfast in our faith in Christ Jesus until the end. Overcoming requires complete dependence upon God for direction, purpose, fulfillment, and strength to follow His plan for our lives (Proverbs 3:5-6). Whether or not your decision is within the will of God or if you wonder if God is pleased with you, God knows our weakness and through His sovereign love for us He works all things according to His purpose and will. I have had my share of ups and downs, struggles, and heartaches in my life and to be honest with you, there were many times, I did not understand why me!

This book, *"Overcomer",* is my life story. As I reflect on my life and all the people whom I have encountered, I realized that it was all part of God's plan for me, for my life, plans to prosper and not to harm me, plans to give me hope and a future (Jeremiah 29:11). God knew I was rough around the edges and had to be refined, and processed, in order for me to walk in my predestined purpose and destiny in this earthly life.

Chapter 1

In the Beginning

My childhood was not a childhood to be envied. Both my parents were immigrants. They crossed to the United States with a dream of having a better life and for their children to have opportunities they did not have growing up in Mexico. We first lived in Texas, where I was born, then we moved to the state of New Mexico, and from there we moved to Arizona. My father was a farmworker, a manual laborer mostly working in the cotton fields, and mother was a stay-home mom. She managed the household and took care of us. As an immigrant family, we moved around a lot. We did not stay long in a certain place, at least not long enough to call it home; not until my parents bought their first and only house in a small town where they finally decided to settle.

I am the third child of eleven children, five boys and six girls. I was a sickly and timid child. My mom told me when I was two years old that I got very sick with a fever. It could not be controlled and ended up at the hospital. She said I almost died. I don't remember her telling me exactly what caused the fever. I do know that growing up I was constantly sick. My parents took me to the doctor and was told I had tonsillitis but with no health insurance, my parents could not afford to take me to the hospital to have them removed. At school, I always found myself in the school nurse office with an upset stomach, sore throat, or fever. Because I was constantly sick, I was pampered a lot by mom. I was always by her side. I think that is why I became so close to her as I grew up. Years later after a lot of gargling with salt and warm water, and mom praying over me, the tonsillitis cleared up.

At an early age, my older sister and I began helping mother around the house, looking out after our younger siblings. We had to grow up quickly and be responsible. We missed out on enjoying our childhood. One of the worst chores for me was washing dirty diapers. Each time it was my turn, the nasty smell would turn my stomach. Back then there was no such thing as disposable diapers and if there were, my parents thought it was a waste of money. It seems like every year there was a new addition to the family. As the family grew it became more difficult for my father to provide any extras for the family. However, he managed to make sure there was always food on the table and a roof over our heads. Back then, the farmers provided housing for their laborers. My dad always made sure the house offered for us to live in was in good condition before he had us move in. He worked long hours each day. I do not recall my father ever missing a day from work. Rain or shine, or in sickness, he would get up early each morning along with mom to prepare his lunch, to go to work out in the fields. Father was not a man of many words nor did he show any emotions or affection. He was very strict with us. Mother was the loving one, reassuring us that even though dad may come across unloving, he did love us in his own way. Once school was out for the summer, we worked in the cotton fields to earn money to purchase our school clothes and school books. This became the norm working out in the cotton fields every summer.

When we first started to go to school, we did not know how to speak English. Those were trying times for us three older kids. Our parents did not allow us to practice the English language at home. The only language allowed to be spoken at home was Spanish. You see, my parents did not know how to speak English. My pronunciation was horrible and I had an accent when I spoke. I used to get ridiculed when I tried to speak English by the kids at school, and eventually even by my younger sibling as well. I remember at grade school, during class, I would hide from the teacher so she could not see me and call my name to stand up and read out loud in front of the class. Each time I got teased by the kids at school, it would take all of me to withhold my tears. I wasn't about to cry in front of them. I could not understand how they could be so mean to me. My mother always taught us to be nice to people, be kind, polite, and respectful. Because of the way the kids at school treated me, I did not like going to school. I stayed mostly to myself during recess. I became an introvert. I withdrew from everybody. I created my own happy world. I had imaginary friends I would play with. At home, mother would see me from the kitchen window playing and talking to myself. She used to tell me what an imagination I have but she didn't know why I stayed to myself. Even in my adolescent years, I never really had any friends. I always felt I had nothing in common with them or did not fit in. Going out to parties and/or drinking did not intrigue me. I grew up being so cautious when I spoke, because I did not want to embarrass myself by mispronouncing words. Even up to this day, I have to stay focused when pronouncing certain words.

All through my childhood up to the seventh grade, we lived isolated, out in the country. There were no neighbors nearby, no children our age to play with, so my brothers and sisters were my friends and rivalries. We would fight, get mad, and at the end of the day make up with each other. We did not have a choice. Mother always made us apologize to each other and be respectful towards each other. Growing up back then had its perks if you were one of the oldest. The younger ones had to do what was told to them but within reason. We grew up believing in God. Mother instilled in us the fear of God. I would listen very intensely. She definitely made an impression on me as far as God was concerned. "God watches every step we take" she would say, "He knows if we are good or bad, and will punish us if we do not behave or lie." I was so fearful of God. I always tried my best to be good and do what I was told. I remember saying to my brothers and sisters not to do this or that or you're going to get in trouble. God is watching. But they wouldn't listen and did their shenanigans behind my mother's back.

I come from a Catholic background. We went to church every Sunday not because I wanted to but I had no choice. It was the only time my parents would take us to town to go to church. As a child, I never understood why we had to stand up, kneel down, stand up, kneel down all through the mass service. I didn't understand the priest. The mass service was in Latin. You had to sit still, not make any noise or else you got in trouble. Mass service was so somber. It became a ritual. Each Sunday it was the same. I used to sit there and wonder where is God? He felt so far away. I never felt the connection spiritually. I quit going to church when I became of age but never stopped reading the bible, praying, or believing in God.

We grew up poor and never knew it. As far as I was concerned, we had everything. We always lived in a nice house, there was food on the table, never went hungry, and had clothes to wear. I remembered when mother would tell us at the dinner table, *"not even the president of the United States is eating what we are eating!"* Hearing that, to us, meant we were living pretty good. We didn't lack anything. Since we lived far from neighbors, we did not compare our lifestyle to anybody else's. Our life was simple and care-free. Those were happy times. Life was good as we knew it...

We moved into town when I was in the eighth grade. Life was so different compared to living out in the country. As we became older, my mom depended on me and my older sister to look after our younger siblings. My older sister did not want any part of it. She was already in high school and had a boyfriend.

She had her own plans and she wasn't going to let anybody ruin them. Right after high school she moved out of the house, moved to Phoenix, and ended up marrying her high school sweetheart. My siblings started to spread their wings, making friends, getting involved in sports, and hanging out. I helped mom make sure all of us did our chores and kept an eye out making sure my brothers and sisters stayed out of trouble.

"I grew up poor and didn't know it."

Chapter 2

Spreading My Wings

After graduating from high school, my first real job besides working in the cotton fields, was working at the Pinal and Gila Counties Legal Aid Office. I was hired as a receptionist. I did not have a clue of what I was doing or how to operate the phone. All I was told to do was to answer the phone and take messages. You see, I never worked in an office setting before. I believe I was hired because the Office Manager saw potential in me and I was very respectful and polite towards her. I was very grateful to be given the opportunity. I was so excited! I applied myself and gave it my best. I wanted her to know that I was dependable, punctual, and willing to learn and do anything that needed to be done. Those work ethics were instilled by my father. He would always tell us to be respectful, responsible, be on time, and do everything to the best of your ability. In other words, do it in excellence! I have always lived by those core work ethics throughout my life. I learned so much that I was promoted to secretary for one of the attorneys. As a secretary, I was inspired to become a legal assistant then eventually be an attorney. That meant I needed to go back to school and pursue my education.

However, it wasn't the right time for me to go back to school. My parents were just making it financially and mom needed help with my brothers and sisters. As the oldest at home, I continued watching over my siblings, taking the role of the authoritarian, and responsibility for them. By doing so, I was excluded from being part of their mischievous behavior. Even though they were just being kids, I had to be the adult. I was constantly making sure that they did their chores at home and school homework, if any. When they misbehaved, I had to discipline them. They were sent to a corner to kneel down and repent for misbehaving. I would tell them that if they did not behave and do good, God was going to punish them. I found myself saying the same thing mom would say to us. As time went by, mom relied on me so much that it became a burden on me. I had assumed the responsibility of a parent without being a parent. I was never invited by my siblings to do things with them. Even still today, when we do get together and they start to reminisce, I just sit there and listen thinking, when did that happen?! I don't remember that. I missed so many memorable moments with my brothers and sisters. You may ask why I took on that role? I did it because I wanted to help mom. I felt obligated. She had done so much for us. She always made sacrifices for us and went without just so that we could have. I remember as a child, I would wake up in the middle of the night and see her sewing dresses for us, using the flour sacks because she did not have money to buy material. The flour sacks came in beautiful flowered fabric. She even made curtains and her own aprons with the flour sack fabrics. She would stay up late, into the early morning and then up again to fix dad his lunch for work. She never complained. I don't remember mom being sick and if she had her days of not feeling well, she never said anything. I loved and admired that woman so much. Her strength and faithfulness in God inspired me.

After leaving my employment at Pinal & Gila Counties Legal Aid Office, I began working at the Arizona Motor Vehicle Division. The pay was much better. I worked there for a year or so, then a position came up that paid even more but was in the Phoenix area. I went ahead and applied for the position after talking with my older sister who lived in Phoenix about the opportunity. She encouraged me and said I could stay with them.

On my first day, I was both nervous and excited. When I got there, I noticed the girls in the office were not friendly. They were sizing me up as I stood there feeling so out of place. Thank God, the lady I was replacing approached me and welcomed me. She was a very sweet old lady ready to retire. She noticed how I was being treated and told me not to pay attention to them. They were upset because an outsider got the position and the promotion was not from within. I was young, naïve, and could not understand it. Three weeks had passed by and the situation in the office had not changed at all. I was being ostracized. They made it very difficult for me to learn what my job entailed. I was being sabotaged. It was clear I was not wanted or welcomed there. I felt so helpless. As I was talking to God to help me handle the situation, tears rolled down my face. It bothered me so much, it was affecting me mentally and physically. After working there for about a month, I became ill. That's how much it affected me. I prayed asking God for guidance and direction. I was at a crossroad. Part of me wanted to stay and stick it out; the other part of me wanted to go back home. After much praying, I decided I needed to go back home.

"They were upset because an outsider got the position and the promotion was not from within."

Chapter 3

Love, Marriage & Family

Going back home was a good move for me. Instead of seeking employment, I applied for an education grant and enrolled at Central Arizona College, a Junior College. I took courses to obtain an Associate Degree in Administration/Criminal Justice System. I was so focused on my studies. I had set a goal to graduate at the end of the two-year term with my degree. While in college, I met my future husband. He was tall, handsome, had an easygoing personality, and was on the basketball team. We started dating. Our relationship gradually became serious. We made plans to marry right after graduation so that both of us could go to Silver City, New Mexico. He had received a basketball scholarship, with an opportunity to pursue his education and I would find employment.

When I decided to go back to school and pursue my education, one of my younger sisters was already in her second year there. We were roommates. She was fortunate enough to get a job as a Dorm Monitor. The education grant I received paid for my tuition, books, and lodging. I ended up working part-time in the Athletic Department as secretary to the Head Basketball Coach. The pay was minimal, but it was better than nothing. We did our best to stretch our money until next payday. However, there were times we ended up running out of personal toiletries before payday. We did not have the financial support from our parents like the other kids. We were on our own. We had to survive somehow. I am ashamed to admit it, but there were times we went into the other girls' rooms to get shampoo, deodorant, or lotion. We only took what we needed if they had extras. To us, it was a blessing that my sister had access to the rooms in her assigned Dorm. Funny, we never thought of it as stealing, but now that I think about it, I guess we were stealing, but out of necessity. I know it doesn't make sense, but I guess God was watching over us.

My second year in college was a little different than the first one. At least I did not have to sneak into the other girls' rooms if I needed any personal toiletries. I was able to maintain my job as secretary to the Head Basketball Coach. My sister decided not to go back to school. I had a very nice girl from Chicago as my roommate. We became close friends. She knew my financial situation and asked if I needed to use some of her toiletries, to go ahead. She said her aunt, who raised her, sends her more than enough money so I did not need to worry. I was so thankful and thanked God for giving me a hand. It was a good year, I stayed focused on my studies.

Graduation was finally here. The day of my graduation was supposed to be one of the most exciting days in my life. After all, it was a big accomplishment. I was the first one from the family to graduate from college. I was so excited! Couldn't wait to see my family witness this monumental event. After the ceremony, my excitement was reduced quickly. The only family members who attended the graduation ceremony were dad, mom, and only one of my sisters. Nobody else came to my graduation. There was no celebration at home, no congratulations from other family members, nothing! What was supposed to be one of my highlights in my life turned out to be a sad moment for me. I was so hurt. I felt like nobody cared enough for me to celebrate with me my accomplishment.

A couple of days later after graduation, I had mustered enough courage to tell my parents I was getting married and moving to Silver City, New Mexico. I told them we wanted to get married right away before the school semester started. Nothing big, just a simple wedding ceremony. My parents were adamant that we have a church ceremony. Before the wedding day, mom and I were in her bedroom and asked me if I was sure this is what I wanted. I said yes. She looked at me and said I was going to have a hard life financially and that we were not going to even be able to afford to buy salt. In our culture, those words were like a curse spoken over my life. I could not believe what I was hearing. Her words were like an arrow piercing through my heart. I was wounded emotionally and hurt by the person I loved the most in my entire life; my mother! I never imagined her saying that to me. Instead of receiving her blessing, I received a curse.

We got married in August 1980, the same summer I graduated and left for Silver City, New Mexico. He continued his education and played basketball for Western New Mexico University. I ended up getting a job at the University at the Registrar's office and became pregnant the same year. My baby girl was born June 2, 1981. Luckily, I was employed and had insurance to pay the hospital and doctor's bills. And yes, it turned out like my mother had said. Financially, we were struggling to make ends meet. There were numerous times when I would go to my quiet place and pray asking God for help and provision. I could not shake off those words spoken by my mother over my life. Years later, I did get the courage to confront my mother and asked her why she said those words over my life. She said she did not remember saying it but she asked for forgiveness for hurting me. I now know that words spoken have power; they are spirit. I try to be mindful of what I say especially when I get upset at someone. Instead of saying the wrong thing, I keep quiet or walk away. I watch what comes out of my mouth because in the Bible it says the tongue has the power of life and death (Proverbs 18:21).

My married life was not what I imagined it to be. After a year and a half into my marriage, I started to see how different my husband and I were. When you are young and start dating everything is wonderful. Each person puts their best foot forward, you feel all giddy inside and think it will be like this forever. You are led by your emotions. Then all of a sudden things aren't quite so wonderful. You start noticing behaviors/things that you did not notice before, attitudes start to change, you don't see things quite the same, your worldviews are different, your faith in God is not at the same level, and priorities are off-balanced. He wanted to spend money to go drinking with his basketball buddies while I was trying to save money for diapers, baby milk, and food. I wanted to go to church on Sundays. He had no desire to go to church. The honeymoon ended quickly and reality settled in. We were struggling financially and there was a lot of tension in our marriage, so we decided that the best thing for us was for me and our baby girl to move back to Arizona while he stayed behind and finished his education. He had approximately six months to go. I stayed with my older sister in Phoenix until I was able to find a job and settle in. I thank God she and her husband opened the door to their home for us.

Yes, it was my cho*ice and my decision* to marry him. In hindsight, I know now I got married out of desperation. I wanted to get away from home and start living my own life, not taking into account the consequences of jumping to the first opportunity! I got married for all the wrong reasons. But God has a way of shedding light on a gloomy situation. The bible says the Lord is my lamp and turns darkness into light (Samuel 22:29). I was blessed to give birth to a beautiful healthy baby girl. She was my salvation and my light in my marriage. I did not believe in divorce. I was determined to try to make it work. Divorce was something that was frowned upon back in those days. Like the saying goes, "you made your bed, now lay with it."

I began to understand what the phrase "unequally yoked" means in 2 Corinthians 6:14 *"Be ye not unequally yoked together with unbelievers: for what fellowship hath righteousness with unrighteousness? And what communion hath light with darkness?"* The Amplified Bible says, *"Do not be unequally bond together with unbelievers [do not make mismatched alliances with them, inconsistent with your faith]. For what partnership can righteousness have with lawlessness?"* A yoke is a wooden bar that joins two oxen to each other and to the burden they pull. An "unequally yoked" team has one stronger ox and one weaker ox, or one taller or one shorter. The weaker or shorter ox would walk more slowly than the taller, stronger one, causing the load to go around in circles. Instead of working together, they are at odds with one another.

This is where my marriage was, like two individuals working against each other, instead of working together as a team. If the truth had to be told, we had nothing in common. And the worst part of attempting to live a Christian life with a non-Christian was going around in circles, especially on how to raise our child. His priorities as a husband were not in alignment with his responsibilities as a family man. He wanted to be married, cared for, and have a place to come to but he also wanted his freedom as a single person, going and coming as he chose. It was not easy, nevertheless, I remained faithful. I prayed each day for strength, patience and prayed for my husband. I would be reminded in Romans 8:25 *"But if we hope for what we do not see, we wait eagerly for it with patience and composure."* This scripture always gave me hope.

Once I moved back to Arizona I was able to find employment where my sister worked. I was the receptionist for a well-known Insurance company. It was not what I preferred but I could not afford to be choosy. I needed to work as soon as possible. I had a baby girl that I was responsible for. After working there for three months, I had saved up enough money to move into an apartment nearby where my sister lived. My husband left the university with only two months left from getting his degree. I still do not know why he never finished his education. His excuse was he missed us but I have a hard time believing that. Luckily, he was able to find a job in no time. We were both working and doing much better financially, at least we were able to pay our monthly bills and stay afloat till payday but our relationship had deteriorated. He kept partying and going out drinking with his buddies. I would dread him coming home each time because I never knew what kind of state of mind he would be in. I remembered one night he came home from one of his drinking sprees with his buddies. He was so upset he threw me out of the apartment in the middle of the night and locked the door. I was so scared and cold. Crying, I banged on the door yelling to let me in. I was so concerned for my baby girl. After banging on the door for at least ten minutes, I ran all the way to my sister's house.

I did not realize I was in an abusive relationship. He had changed so much. It was as if I did not know him. Instead of feeling protected I was in fear most of the time. He even left us. He went back home to be with his family. I was so embarrassed. I felt like a failure as a woman. I could not tell my parents or siblings what I was going through. I kept it to myself and kept praying asking God to help me! He was gone for a month or so. I didn't hear from him nor received any financial help from him. Thank God I was still working at the Insurance Company.

In the meantime, my sister and her husband lived in Georgia. He was in the military getting ready to be deployed to Germany and didn't want to leave my sister and the baby in Georgia alone away from family, they decided to move to Arizona prior to his deployment. They got an apartment in the same Apartment Complex I lived in. My brother-in-law left for Germany and my sister Lupe was able to get employment at the same Insurance Company I worked at. During lunch breaks I would encourage her to go out with the girls her age to lunch, to hang out with them. She said to me that she wanted to hang out with me. She wanted to be my friend, not just my sister. We became very close regardless of our age difference. We helped each other financially and gave each other the emotional support we needed. Together, we stretched our money until next payday, we carpooled, took turns buying gas, and combined our dinner meals. There were times we would not eat at work. On occasions, we would treat ourselves and go to What-a-Burger during our lunch break. I remember one day we were eating at What-a-Burger, sitting outside and the weather was just perfect. In Arizona, you do not normally have nice weather to enjoy a meal outdoors. This particular day was different. As we were conversing, my sister said, *"Maria, if something ever happens to me, please make sure my daughter gets my wedding rings when she turns 21 years old or right before she marries."* Her daughter, at that time, was only one and a half years old. I looked at her with bewilderment and said, *"Why are you talking about this?"* She said, *"I'm serious. Please promise me."* I responded, *"Okay, I promise, but can we talk about something else?"* We finished our meal and headed back to work.

"God has a way of shedding light
on a gloomy situation."

Chapter 4

Grief Strikes

A week later, on October 15, 1984, is a date I will never forget. It was Monday morning and it was my week to drive to work. The alarm clock woke me up. I looked at the time and it was 6:00 a.m. For the first time ever, for some inexplicable reason, I did not feel like going to work. I rolled over to go back to sleep then I remembered, it's my turn to drive and Lupe is going to come knocking on the door asking what is going on. An hour later, a little bit after 7:00 a.m, I heard a knock at the door. I got out of bed and went to open the door and my sister was standing there. She looked so beautiful wearing a light blue blouse, had a little bit of makeup on, just enough to enhance her beauty. She was surprised to see me still in my pajamas and said, *"You're still in your pajamas! Aren't you going to work?"* I said, *"Sister, I'm sorry but for some reason I don't feel like going to work. Could you please just let them know I'm not feeling well."* She said, *"Okay. I'll let them know."* I responded, *"Thank you sis! You look so beautiful. Give me a hug."* We hugged each other and I told her how much I love her. She left. I went back to bed. About five minutes later or so, I heard loud knocks on the door more like banging the door. Immediately I jumped out of bed and went to the door. As I opened the door, it was my older sister crying hysterically. The only word coming out of her mouth was *"Sister, Sister!* I tried to get her to calm down but was unable to. I ran outside into the parking lot, went around the complex building, saw my sister's car, and the driver side door opened. As I approached the car, I saw my sister on the ground bleeding, unconscious, and not responding. I held her in my arms praying till the paramedics arrived. While the paramedics were attending to her, an Air Evac Life Team was dispatched and she was air-evac to St. Joseph Hospital. Through all this horrific ordeal, I kept my composure. I knew I had to remain strong. I was operating in my survival instinct mode. At least that's what I thought. Little did I know it was my God who discharged his angels (Psalm 91:11) to guard and carry me, giving me comfort, strength and peace, while giving me fortitude to ***overcome*** this nightmare.

At the hospital, all of my brothers and sisters arrived with the exception of our parents. They had gone to Nogales, Mexico earlier that morning. We had no way of communicating with them. While I stood there watching my brothers and sisters with tears in their eyes, in distraught and disbelief, I was led by the Holy Spirit to pray silently while struggling to hold back my own tears. Some were sitting down, others pacing back and forth, while others exited the doors of the hospital back and forth. We were all waiting to hear from the doctor. It was so surreal. Is this really happening? Did someone really stab our sister? How can harm come to someone who never afflicted pain to anybody, to a caring loving person, someone who only did good? There were so many questions going through my mind and emotions were on high alert. Finally, the doctor approached us, took us into a small room and informed us that our sister had passed away. She had suffered numerous stab wounds, lost a lot of blood, and also had a broken arm. Screams of desperation and weeping broke out. My brothers and sisters were in so much pain. All I could say was *My God, my God help us!* A few minutes later, I got this bright idea and said let's pray. They all looked at me and I heard them say, *pray?? You want us to pray? Our sister just died! And you want us to pray? Pray to who? What kind of a God would allow this to happen to our sister?*

They exited the room and went into the hallway. I asked the nurse who was on standby if I could go in to see my sister. She took me into the room where she laid. Tears started rolling down my face as I touched her and said my goodbyes. I exited the room, as I was passing my brothers and sisters, I noticed two Phoenix Detectives were talking to them, but I kept walking and exited the hospital. I crossed the street and went to the parking lot and stood under a big tall green beautiful tree. I wanted to be alone in my grief and looked up into the sky talking to my God, so I could ask why did this have to happen? All of a sudden, I heard a voice from behind me. I turned around to see who it was. It was one of the Detectives. He asked me if I was one of the sisters. I said yes. He said I have something for you I think you should have. He extended his hand toward me and as I reached my hand out, he placed my sister's wedding rings on my hand! He walked away. I held those rings closed to my chest as tears rolled down my face and looked up into the sky and said, *"Sister, I made you a promise and I will keep it."* I could not believe how those rings ended up in my hand. Sometimes, there are things that cannot be explained. You just have to continue to walk in faith, search deep inside, and trust in God no matter what happens. Lamentations 3:22-23 in the New International Version: *"Because of the Lord's great love we are not consumed, for his compassions never fail. They are new every morning; great is your faithfulness."*

After the Detectives finished asking questions, we all decided to leave the hospital together and go to our parents' house, about an hour drive away. When we got there, we waited, wondering how on earth are we going to tell them that one of their children is dead...murdered? They are going to know something is wrong when they see all of our cars parked in front of their home, especially on a weekday. That was the hardest and toughest thing we ever had to do.

My parents returned back home late in the afternoon. Immediately, mom looked at us and her face told me she knew she was about to hear the worst news a parent could receive.

We told both of them at the same time. All we could do was comfort them and each other. It was too painful for me to see a mother grieve for her child. How can someone make sense out of this? You cannot. The Bible says to turn to him in the time of trouble, for God is our refuge and strength (Psalm 46:1). And that is what I had to do; put my faith in God, for solace, comfort and strength.

After the funeral, I went back to my apartment. I wanted to cry, but couldn't. I asked God privately why did this have to happen? I needed an answer. As I opened the bible it opened to Isaiah 57:1 in the New International Version: *"The righteous perish, and no one ponders it in his heart; devote men are taken away, and no one understands that the righteous are taken away to be spared from evil."* When I read that verse, I felt such peace and comfort consuming me. I wept and understood why. That was the last time I wept for my sister!

It was so difficult going back to work. I missed my sister so much. Everywhere I went and turned it reminded me of her. A month later after the passing of my sister, I received a letter from the Arizona Department of Corrections. I opened it and it stated that I had been scheduled to take the written examination and psychological test for employment. Mind you, I had submitted my application for quite some time that I had forgotten. But my God, He made a way for me. He shows mercy and moves in compassion. This was my opportunity to change my place of employment. I was so excited I had been accepted to test for employment with the State. I went to take my written examination and the psychological test. A couple of weeks later, I received notification that I had passed and had a starting date of November 17, 1984, to report to the Arizona Department of Corrections Academy, a month later after my sister's death.

I had to report in uniform. However, there was a problem. I did not have the money to purchase my uniform gear and shoes. I decided to go to one of the uniform stores to get an idea how much money I was going to need for the uniform, belt, and shoes. It came out to approximately one hundred dollars. I did not have the money. I went to my quiet place and prayed asking God how I am going to get the money? He put it in my heart to ask one of my sisters to loan me the money. I was not accustomed to asking for money or anything from anybody, so it wasn't easy for me. I knew I had to put my pride aside and humble myself and ask. I finally got the courage to ask for the money and I promised I would pay it back with my first paycheck. I went to the uniform store, tried the uniform on, stood in front of a full-length mirror and could not believe it was me standing there wearing a Correctional officer's uniform.

In the interim, the person who had murdered my sister was caught and in custody. He had a criminal record for sexual assault and rape. He had just completed his parole and had served time in the Arizona Department of Corrections (ADOC). This individual was living in the same Apartment Complex we lived in. Evidently, he had been watching us, getting familiar with our routine. When the police searched the immediate area of the crime scene, they also searched each apartment at the Complex until they got to the apartment where they found the knife, which still had blood on it, and the police was able to get fingerprints from the knife. The blood matched my sister's. The Phoenix Police Department immediately activated a man hunt once his identity was established and he was apprehended two days later.

Sometimes, there are things
that cannot be explained.

Chapter 5

Moving On

My first day to report to the Arizona Department of Corrections Academy was finally here. As I stood there dressed in my uniform, before exiting the apartment, I took one last long look in the mirror, admiring myself in my correctional officer's uniform. For the first time in my life I felt proud of myself. I was wearing a uniform that represented a part of the law enforcement field. I felt God was smiling at me. I wanted God to be proud and pleased with me. My heart was jumping with joy and thankfulness! At the same time, I was very nervous of the unknown and the unexpected. November 17, 1984, was the beginning of a new chapter in my life!

The academy lasted six weeks. Those six weeks were very intense, challenging, and exhilarating. A day before graduation, we were advised by our senior academy instructor of our unit assignments. I was assigned to Perryville Complex, Santa Maria Unit, a female unit. It housed inmates of custody levels from minimum to maximum. Upon reporting to work, we were told we would be assigned to 40 hours on-the-job-training from 8am-4pm prior to starting our assigned shift. I was assigned to swing shift, which are the hours from 1pm to 9pm ,with Tuesday and Wednesday as my days off.

I was very grateful for being hired with the State of Arizona but it was very difficult for me to overcome this fear that took hold of me after the death of my sister. I was so fearful coming home each night by myself, especially, when I pulled up to the parking lot at the Apartment Complex. I remember telling my husband please be home when I get home and keep an eye out for me in the parking lot. I would literally stay in my car for at least 15 to 20 minutes because I was afraid of being attacked by some stranger hiding in the bushes. Finally, when I was able to muster up the courage to get out of the car, I would run to the door breathing hard. My husband was not home most of the time when I got home, so the times he would be, he'd ask me what's wrong. I just looked at him and wondered if he did not understand I'm fearful something might happen to me? I knew that unconsciously I was afraid that what happened to my sister could happen to me. I did not feel safe and unknowingly allowed this fear to take over me and control me.

Working the swing shift helped us save money at the Daycare Center. Our baby girl was only there 2 hours daily. My husband would pick her up after he got off work. However, I worried because instead of staying home with her, he would take her to the park, stay out late playing basketball, or be at his friend's house hanging out and drinking. He could not understand why I would make a big fuss over it. Remember, I mentioned earlier how my husband and I were "unequally yoked", and we both had different views of parenting.

I remembered one day, someone very close to me, a family member told me I should lighten up and quit being so rigid. This individual said I don't think your husband will put his own daughter in harm's way. I said *really?* What if it was your baby girl would you feel the same way? How can this person stand there and accuse me of being rigid? I was concerned about my baby's safety and welfare. A responsible father does not take his three-year-old baby out late in the evening just because he wants to play basketball or hang out with his buddies playing dominoes and have a couple of drinks. I could not make him understand that drinking and driving with our baby girl in the car was irresponsible. My marriage was taking its toll on me. I was so unhappy; I was suffering in silence. I kept praying asking God for guidance and direction in my marriage, to protect my baby girl, and to change my husband's way of thinking. The word of God always gave me comfort and hope. It filled me with peace as I trusted in Him that one day things would change for the better (Romans 15:13 AMP).

This living arrangement continued for six months until my probationary period was over. By then I would be eligible to put in for a different shift and days off. In the meantime, I applied myself in learning everything I needed to learn as a Correctional officer. Each day was different. We never knew if we were going to have a quiet day or some kind of incident, for example a fight, a heated verbal confrontation, medical transport, or an incident which required a total lockdown. Working in a correctional setting was like being in a totally different world. I never foresaw myself working in a correctional female institution or working in a correctional setting for that matter.

I saw so much sorrow, brokenness, despair, anger, and loneliness. Some women pretended to be tough and tried to intimidate other inmates and new officers. I remember walking the yard for the first time, from far away I saw what appeared to be a man. In my mind, I asked myself what is that man doing in a female unit. As I got closer, I realized it was a woman who looked like a man, acted like a man, mannerism and all. I played it off and acted like it was nothing. I asked my training officer to explain that to me and he told me that I would be seeing a lot of this. There were some women into homosexuality, the ones who take the role of a man, called a "dike" in a lesbian relationship. Some women even though they are not homosexuals, they get into it because of the feeling of loneliness and the need of belonging to. The women knew it's against rule regulations to engage in homosexual activities, so they would not display such affections in front of officers. Some tried to be sneaky. This was so new to me. I was never exposed, saw, or heard of this. I lived a sheltered life and was very naïve in the things of the world.

In the academy, we were taught to be fair and consistent in our dealings with inmates and to be observant at all times. I took that to heart. Even though they were inmates they were also human beings and I treated them as such with respect and dignity. I was raised if you want respect, you show respect. When assigned to the housing units or the yard, I watched who they hung out with, got familiar with their character, their routine, and who was running things within. For the most part, it was very rare that I had any issues with the inmates. Although, I remember this incident very well. I was assigned to a housing unit. At that time, I was still working the swing shift. I was getting ready to conduct a health and welfare check, when an inmate came up to the office door demanding her mail. I told her the mail would be passed out after I'm done conducting a health and welfare check. She got enraged with me and started calling me all sorts of filthy names and I didn't have a clue what those words meant! I was not familiar with such profanity. You see, throughout my entire life, I did not curse or use profanity words. I looked at her as she kept on and finally when she realized that I was not reacting to her behavior, she stopped, looked at me and said, *"F...king Drake, you're different. Any other officer would have put me on lockdown and written me up."* Unbeknownst to me, her issue was not that she did not get her mail when she asked me, she was having serious family issues and it was her only way of letting some of the anger out. Because I did not react to her outburst, this inmate never again gave me any problems or disrespected me. As a matter of fact, she was one of the inmates who called the shots in the yard. The word got out that I was an upright officer. If asked something and I did not know the answer, I would tell them that I need to find out and let them know. I was not one of those who blew them off. With me it was either yes or no. I had built a rapport with the inmates and for the most part they listened to me. They kept their cells cleaned and in compliance. Thank God I never had any major issues with any inmate.

Even the staff noticed that in my dealings with inmates, I never used profanity and always treated the inmates with dignity. I remember the day we got a new Captain assigned to our unit. I must admit he was very good looking and there were quite a few female officers drooling over him. After a couple of weeks being there, he began to come to me as the go-to-person. One afternoon, I walked into his office. He immediately removed his legs off the desk and sat up. In his office, there were at least two sergeants and three officers talking and laughing with him. They noticed his demeanor changed as soon as I walked in and one of the Sergeant said a couple of curse words as they were talking. The captain immediately corrected her and told her not to use profanity in front of me. She asked him why? He said Officer Drake is not like you guys. She is different. In a way, it made me feel good that he recognized me in that manner but at the same time what he said did not sit well with the others in the room.

A lot of the women incarcerated were there because of their husbands or boyfriends. They committed a crime due to fear, intimidation, or extortion from their husbands, baby's daddy or boyfriends. There was so much brokenness, hurt, confusion, low self-esteem, loneliness, despair, and anger. I was able to relate to them. I listened, gave them hope that they could change for the better, and to believe in themselves. I encouraged them to strive to improve by taking advantage of the programs being offered to them, to enroll in programs on how to acquire life skills and parental skills, and for those who did not have a diploma to work towards their GED, and most importantly to read the Bible and pray.

I remember one of the women, she was in her early twenties and had severe issues. Her way of dealing with life was self-inflicting pain either by cutting herself and/or banging her head on the wall. She had such low self-esteem that she was convinced she was not capable of accomplishing anything, and did not have the confidence. I would always give her a word of encouragement till she finally started believing she could do it. She enrolled in a class and worked very hard. She couldn't wait for me to report to work to show me her progress. I would always give her kudos and encourage her to stay focused. This inmate was among many who felt unworthy, unloved, and had low self-esteem.

Chapter 6

Our Son

Two years later, I got pregnant. I was still struggling in my marriage and here I was having another child. My husband was happy he was going to have a son. For a moment, I thought maybe this would change him. He would grow up and become more responsible as a husband and family man. During my third trimester, I was assigned to Main Control away from inmate contact. I was hoping to work almost up to my due date but had some complications. I was experiencing premature labor pains and the doctor recommended I be placed on bedrest, so I applied for Family and Medical Leave.

The hope I had for my husband to grow up and become more responsible vanished the day I went into labor. The labor pains started late in the afternoon becoming more intense in the early evening. I called my sisters to let them know I was heading to the hospital. Two of my sisters came along. On the way to the hospital my husband told me he was going to drop me at the hospital and go to the dinner his company was having that evening. He figured I would still be in labor by the time he returned back to the hospital. I could not believe what I heard. Good thing my labor pains were so intense that I did not pay much attention to what he said. When we got to the hospital, I was taken to the maternity ward and when the nurse on call checked me, she told my husband the baby was coming. We needed to get me to the delivery room immediately, hoping the doctor will arrive before this baby makes an entrance into this world.

Maria's son, **SirTerry** at 8 months

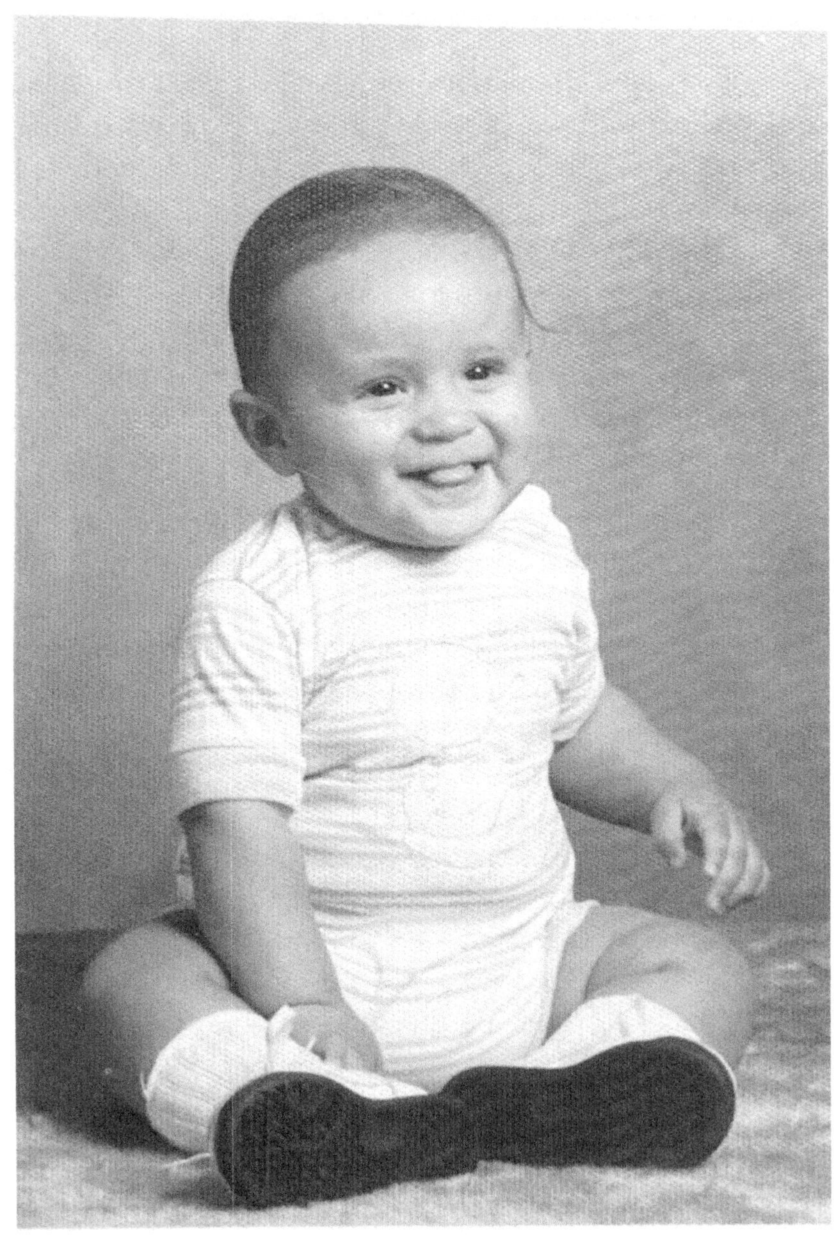

On December 8, 1986 at 9:15 p.m. my baby boy was born! After our son was born, my husband left for the company's dinner. I was so full of joy at the birth of our son that it didn't matter to me if my husband was there or not. I was so happy, my world seemed complete. I was blessed with two healthy children. My children became my world.

A few days after being released from the hospital, I became aware that I was not going to have enough annual and sick leave to cover the time I was going to be out on maternity leave. Therefore, I was forced to go back to work a lot sooner than expected. Bills were piling up. In the midst of all this, my husband decided to go to visit his family in Indiana with no regard to our financial situation. I was left with the responsibility of caring for two children, taking them to the Daycare Center, figuring out how I was going to buy diapers, food, gas, and pay the rent. It was a very difficult time I was going through. I had no idea how I was going to manage. I cried out to God for help! My reliance on God was my hope that somehow, someway I was going to make it through.

After six years working at Perryville Complex, I decided to transfer to Florence Complex. I wanted to be closer to family, closer to my parents, in hopes of getting some emotional support and help in daycare for my children while I went to work. Who can be a better babysitter than their own grandmother, I thought! I shared my thoughts with my husband. To my surprise, he agreed even though it meant he would be driving an hour to and from work. We purchased a small house across the railroad tracks, once used to be HUD homes for lower income families. A housing developer was renovating the houses and selling at an affordable price. We applied for the loan; we were approved but were asking for a closing cost of $1500. I asked my father if he could give me the money as a gift and I would pay him back. I was so happy he agreed. In the meantime, my transfer went through and I was able to coordinate the start work date a week after moving into our new home. It all worked out. I was so happy and full of joy! It was my first home, no more apartment, and close to family. I thanked God that my dream had come true. My family circle was complete. I had two beautiful children, a new house, and a job I enjoyed!

In September of 1990, I started working at Florence Complex. I was assigned to North Unit, a minimum male security yard. This was new to me as I had never worked in a male facility. Right away I noticed the difference compared to a female unit. The biggest difference was, the male inmates stayed within their own race as opposed to the female inmates mingled with other races. I remembered being assigned to the Chow Hall (cafeteria) security and as the male inmates entered, I noticed all whites sat together, all blacks together, all Mexicans together, and so on. It threw me for a loop because I did not understand why. So, I asked the other officer who was with me and he said that's just how it is in the penitentiary. The male inmates stick with their own race for survival. I was still confused. I knew there was much I had to learn in this new environment!

I applied myself each day and completed my assigned assignments to the best of my ability, getting to know who is who out in the yard, who are the heads in each race, who calls the shots out in the yard, and ensuring rules and regulations were being followed. Even the officers I worked with carried themselves differently. They had vulgar mouths. Everything that came out of their mouths were curse words. That did not sit well with me. At one point, I had to tell a group of officers to please not use profanity around me and that I did not appreciate it. I remember one of the officers making a remark saying *"What do you expect? Look at where we work."* I simply replied, *"Just because we are in a correctional setting does not give us the license to use profanity. We should treat each other with respect.*

Those inmates are also human beings and should be treated with dignity. They are already paying for their crimes to society by being here."

After that, I noticed I was being treated differently. For the most part, the majority of the officers were respectful of my request. I had to take a stance and not allow myself to be dehumanized. Time went by and one morning my immediate supervisor and I were talking. He said I had been in this business a long time now and he mentioned that he had never come across someone like me, mentioning that I was different. He told me that I was the type of person that people will like or not like. Out of curiosity, I asked him what he meant by that. He said I set the standards of what is expected from them without even knowing. You do not hang out in the yard office; you are out there in the yard doing your job and that forces them to be out there too. I did not know if I should take it as a compliment or not. However, I remained true to myself.

In Loving Memory of **“SirTerry”** (pictured here: 4 yrs. old)

Chapter 7

My Worst Nightmare

For the first time in a long time, I was happy. Each day after work I couldn't wait to get home to prepare dinner and spend time with my two beautiful children. They were so different but loved the same. Each night, I made sure they bathed and brushed their teeth. Right before bedtime, my son at a very young age would yell *"Say a blessing mom!"* I would enter his room, give him the blessing, and as I prayed over him, I would always get this premonition that he was not going to be with me long. I would see a car accident. Tears would roll down my face as I prayed asking God to protect him. There was never a day I did not ask God to protect my son and daughter, to keep them safe.

My mother's birthday was coming up. My siblings and I were planning a birthday party for her. Friday the day before her birthday, my four-year-old son and I went shopping to buy mom her birthday gift. My daughter did not come with us, as she was in school. That day was one of the most joyful times I've had in a long time. We ended up buying mom her favorite perfume. The next day, I went to work feeling very excited because it was mom's birthday and we were going to gather at her house to celebrate. When I got home, my daughter had her brother all dressed up ready to go. He, on the other hand, complained that his sister did not comb his hair like he likes it. I remember I lifted him up and sat him on the countertop next to the bathroom sink. I wet his hair and combed it like he liked it. Between you and me it looked the same but it made him happy. Before leaving the house, I took his toy four-wheeler and placed it in the trunk of the car. I thought he could entertain himself riding it in mom's yard along with his little cousins. My husband had to work that day so he was not able to attend. We got to mom's house and the birthday celebration had already started. Everybody was in the front yard. Mom's house had a big front yard so whenever we gathered it would be right there. The music was playing, meat was on the grill, and the kids were running all over the yard.

I was sitting conversing with the sisters and mom, and my son came to me and whispered in my ear *"they won't let me ride my bike."* I told him not to worry, they will soon get tired and he'll have the bike all to himself. A few minutes later, I turned to see where he was and I saw him on the bike exiting out onto the street. At that moment, I froze, my life went into slow motion.As he exited the driveway, I saw a SUV coming down the street, hit my son and dragged him about 75 yards before it stopped. Two of my brothers grabbed me and held me down. They did not want me to see him under the SUV. The police and paramedics arrived and immediately dispatched an Air Evac LifeTeam to air-vac my son to the hospital. My son did not make it to the hospital. He died as he was being air-vac. My whole world turned upside down at that moment. I remember entering the hospital room where he was. His left side of his small face was bandaged. He was laying there lifeless. All I could do was take his small hands and place them on my face. Never had I felt so helpless. I was not able to do anything to bring my son back! As I cried the only words coming out of my mouth was *My God, My God!* After I cried all I could, my eyes were so dried and hurting from crying, I left the room feeling like something had died inside of me. I was numb, in disbelief, and probably in shock. January 21, 1991 was supposed to be a birthday celebration not a tragic event!

The funeral arrangements are vague, I don't recall crying ever again for my son. After his death, I kept having recurring dreams of him. The dreams were always practically the same. I would find myself searching for my son. Each time I found him, he was playing and after calling his name, he would look up towards where I was with a smile or laugh, waving at me. I never saw him sad or crying. He appeared to be happy, having a good time. It was I who was distraught because he was not with me and I wanted to take him home with me. I had this dream over and over for many years, it felt like the movie "GroundHog Day." Each morning I would wake up so depressed, exhausted, and lifeless not wanting to face life but my God, he kept me! He kept me from falling apart and giving up. I prayed every single day asking God to help me, comfort me, and to give me strength. I needed to be strong for my daughter. There were times that instead of praying, I would talk to God. I questioned why this is happening to me. I begged to understand. I felt like I was going crazy. I was a walking dead woman. It's a wonder that I was able to be functional at work!

After the accident, there was an ongoing investigation. The driver of the SUV was a female. Evidently, she had been drinking and had two small children in the vehicle with her. She was arrested. One day while I happened to be home, two detectives came to the house. They wanted to know if I was going to press charges on the woman driver. Without hesitation, I said no. That will not bring my son back. She will have to live with what she did for the rest of her life. Besides, her two children need her. The two detectives stood there speechless for a few minutes and then asked me if I was sure that's what I wanted to do. I replied yes. After that, I never thought of that woman, never saw her or felt any hate towards her. I believe God protected my heart from getting bitter and from getting revenge.

God protected my heart from getting bitter.

Chapter 8

The Final Straw

The death of our son put a huge strain on our marriage. My husband started drinking a lot more, was not coming home everyday after work, and there was hardly any communication between us. The times he would come home from work, he would go straight to shower, get dressed, and out again. If dinner was prepared and served on the table, he would just say he's not hungry and leave. His drinking became worse to the point where he was not helping with the bills. Our relationship was deteriorating more and more each day. I remained faithful to my God, praying to turn around my situation, and to help me. I felt I was sinking deeper and deeper in a hole. I wanted to scream, to yell, to throw the towel in, and not give a heck about anything. But, I couldn't. Each time I looked at my daughter, I kept asking God to give me the strength to move forward, to direct my footsteps in the right direction, and to make the right decision concerning my marriage. I felt so alone and deserted. I did not have the emotional support system I needed as I grieved the loss of my son from my husband or family.

Eventually, the turning point that caused me to file for divorce was when I came home around 11:30 p.m. from a prayer meeting with my mother. Of all nights, my husband decides to come home. As we pulled up, I remember telling mom that my husband is home. Deep inside I was happy. Mom dropped me off and when I entered the house, it was dark. I heard my husband asking where I had been. Before I could answer him, I felt blows on my head. He was punching me with both fists like I was a punching bag. All I can remember is, trying to cover my head with my hands.

When I woke up, I was in my bed. I had a horrible headache. My husband was sitting on a chair. He said I had been sleeping for three days. For three days I was unconscious and he did not think to take me to the hospital! I rolled over, looked at him, and by the grace of God, I got the courage to tell him in a stern voice to pack his belongings and leave. If he was not gone within the next hour, I was going to report him to the police and file charges. He packed his belongings and left. I managed to call work to speak with my immediate supervisor. I explained to him what had happened to me and why I had not called in. Thank God he was very understanding and told me to take as much time that I needed to recover. I went to the bathroom and looked at myself in the mirror. I could not recognize myself. My face was swollen and bruised. I cried until I could cry no more! I kept thanking God for my daughter not being home to see this. She was visiting her cousin in Phoenix. It was at that moment that I knew in my heart that my marriage after thirteen years had come to an end.

It took a very long time to come to terms with what had happened to me. Each time I thought about it, it felt so surreal. How could this happen to me? First, my child is taken. Secondly, my marriage is dissolved. The person who was supposed to be my protector, my covering, had physically assaulted me. I never imagined losing one of my children and my marriage ending like this. I was broken, afraid, felt like a failure, rejected, not worthy and my self-esteem had plummeted. I just wanted to sleep my life away. Depression kicked in. There was not a single night that I did not cry out to my Lord God! I couldn't understand why this was happening to me. All my life, even as a little girl, I always tried to be good, do good, so I could be liked and please God. I felt all alone in the world. One particular night, I even asked God why he had deserted me. After saying that I heard a voice saying *I have not deserted you or abandoned you.* Remember when you were seven years old and you were in church kneeling down. You had your eyes closed and when you opened your eyes, you saw what appeared to be smoke in the atmosphere and it consumed you and you fell. It was I who consumed you preparing you for such a time as this. After hearing this, I cried until I felt a peaceful feeling come over me.

The fear that I mentioned earlier had overcome me completely. It kept me in prison in my own house. It had me paralyzed. On my days off, I made sure I took care of all of my errands during the day or I was home from dinner and movies with my daughter before nightfall. Once it was dark outside, I locked myself in the house. By the grace of God, each morning I was able to get up, get dressed and report to work. Working at Corrections kept me from thinking about the personal problems I was going through. My focus was on issues at hand. Work kept me going. I was like a drill sergeant. Inmates and staff thought I had served in the military by the way I carried on. I was hard-nosed. I expected inmates to be in compliance, follow all the rules, and keep their housing area clean at all times. But at the same time, both inmates and staff knew I was fair and always professional. At the end of each day, some of my peers would always invite me to join them for a drink. I would tell them that I do not drink but they always insisted I hang out with them. I never did. It just didn't feel right. Hanging out at the bars was not me. And I never shared with anybody what I was going through.

*It was I who consumed you,
preparing you for such a time as this.*

Chapter 9

Divine Promotion

In 1993, my divorce was finally finalized. It took me at least four to five months to file for divorce because I did not have the money. I had to humble myself and ask one of my sisters if I could borrow the money. Told her I would pay her back as soon as I could. I was hurting financially, struggling to make ends meet. I was stuck with all the bills my husband and I had accumulated. I was robbing from Peter to pay Paul, juggling bills around, and the bill collectors were calling the house twenty-four hours a day. It got to the point where I stopped answering the phone. I did not want to check the mailbox. All that was there were letters from bill collectors threatening me to pay or else my paycheck would be garnished. It got so bad that I finally swallowed my pride and mentioned my situation to one of my sisters.

She asked me if I had ever thought of filing bankruptcy. I said no. When she mentioned that, I really felt like a failure and embarrassed. She looked at me and said there was nothing to be ashamed of and that it happens to the best of people. She said she had to do it and the process was painless. Once she explained the process, I agreed. She made my appointment and went with me. During my interview with the attorney, he said that I most definitely qualified. I was thankful and relieved that the bill collectors would not be able to garnish my paycheck, and at the same time was so embarrassed. I was thinking what people would think of me since I had to file for bankruptcy. My credit had gone out the window!

I remembered one day coming home from work I noticed that the back door of my house had been broken. I walked inside the house and it had been ransacked! My heart sank. I broke out in tears! I could not believe what I was seeing. I walked into each room and everything was out of place, whoever did it left a mess. It appeared nothing was taken but they were looking for something specific. I felt so violated! I felt emotions I had never felt before. At the same time, I was very relieved and thankful my daughter was not home. A month or so later, I experienced another incident. Someone had broken the back window by the dining area. This time my television and stereo were missing. Again, very thankful my daughter was not home. She was still at school. My daughter's friend came over and helped me put a board up to cover the broken window. It was too late to call or have someone replace the glass window. I will always be forever grateful to my daughter's friend for helping me.

After the second incident, I decided to get a security alarm installed in hope of deterring any future break-ins. Unfortunately, I had one more attempted break-in. The alarm went off and the police showed up in time to scare away whoever was attempting to break-in. I was so beside myself. I could not stop thinking, *why is all this happening to me, Lord? Why?* Once again, I felt so helpless, so alone, and vulnerable. If the walls of that particular house could speak, they would tell you how many times I cried out in despair! I felt that no matter how much I prayed, my prayers were falling on deaf ears.

I had been working in Corrections for eight to nine years, volunteering in special assignments, and working in every area within the unit. I had no desire to be promoted. I was content in being a correctional officer. One night, I was sound asleep when I dreamt seeing myself walking the yard in my starch ironed uniform, my hair in compliance and my shoes shined. In that dream, I saw myself wearing sergeant stripes on both of my sleeves. I woke up in amazement. I said *Lord , I do not want to become a sergeant. I don't want that responsibility.* At that time, the Department was taking applications for Sergeant positions. I kept ignoring this inner feeling, this push, to apply. I felt I wasn't ready. I had too much going on in my personal life and I didn't need additional work stress. But, something inside of me kept pushing me to apply. I finally gave in and applied. I said to myself what do I have to lose? I either pass the written test or not.

When the test day arrived, I took the written test and walked out of the testing room feeling relieved. There, it's over! Two weeks later I was contacted by the Personnel office that I had passed the written test and now I needed to be scheduled for the Oral Board. A month later, the Personnel office distributed the Sergeants list to the Executive Personnel statewide and to all of the Deputy Wardens. I got a call from the Major at the Florence Complex congratulating me for making the Sergeants list and placing number 2 statewide and number one at the complex level. I could not believe it! I kept thinking it had to be God! How in the world was I able to concentrate mentally during the written test and oral board considering what I was going through in my personal life? I saw myself as a sergeant in a dream and now it was a reality! The Major who called me not only congratulated me but offered me a Sergeant's position at Complex with weekends and holidays off. Now I knew God was in the midst of all this because it's very rare for someone who is promoted to sergeant is offered a position at Complex and is not assigned to a unit working graveyard shift. I thanked God for watching over me and having his hand in my life. It also meant an increase on my paycheck!

Becoming a supervisor was scary at first. I was nervous, I did not know how my subordinates were going to accept me or my peers for that matter. I knew I had to win them over, to gain their trust and respect. I always carried myself in a professional manner and tried to be fair with everybody. I never expected my staff to do something I would not do. I tried to lead by example and empowered them to do their job. I never thought of myself as being different from other supervisors but that is what I was told by staff and even as an officer I was told I was different. They told me that I stood out among other officers, I represented with authority and had a commanding presence. I did not see myself like that. I was just being me; a Mexican girl who grew up being ridiculed for speaking with an accent, shy, timid, who treated people with respect, and who was instilled to do everything in excellence. Because of my core work ethics instilled in me, doing everything in excellence, I set high standards and expectations on my staff. There was accountability. Some liked it and some didn't. I tried to be respectable, approachable, and cordial with everybody I had contact with.

As I look back, I now understand why I was told I was different. It was the anointing I was carrying that made me stand out. God had given me the anointing of wisdom and favor. *"But you have an anointing from the Holy One [you have been set apart, specially gifted and prepared by the Holy Spirit], and all of you know [the truth because He teaches us, illuminates our minds, and guards us from error"* (1 John 2:20). The anointing gave me direction and in moments of decisions, the anointing gave me a spirit of wisdom to know what to do and to do or say the right thing. With the anointing, God will make things happen that we could never make happen on our own. God had His hand on me. Because God had His hand on me, I knew it had to be God's favor in my life; He cleared the way for me to be promoted, it was God who gave me the divine promotions throughout my career in spite of my brokenness.

My career was starting to flourish while I was still struggling with the hard knocks life had given me. I had lost my identity and my sense of worth along the way. But I knew I had to stay in faith and believe in God's plan for me. In 3 John 1:2 (AMP) says, *"Beloved, I pray that in every way you may succeed and prosper and be in good health [physically,], just as [I know] your soul prospers [spiritually]."* I stood on that word that God was going to prosper me, heal me emotionally, physically, and spiritually.

The increase in pay was a blessing. No more counting pennies when going to the grocery store. I remember one time I was buying groceries and the cashier told me my total and I felt my face getting red from embarrassment. I did not have enough money to pay and had to tell her to put some back. After, I walked towards the car with my groceries and I said, *"Lord, I know one of these days, I will be able to buy whatever and as much groceries without being concerned of not having enough money in my pocket."* I said it with much conviction and faith. I had even contemplated many times to quit working just to withdraw my pension and get back on my feet. But each time that thought came to my mind, I always heard a soft voice saying *hang in there, do not quit.*

It was the anointing I was carrying that made me stand out.

Chapter 10

Unexpected Provision

Even though my family never came to visit or to see how I was doing or if I needed anything, God would always come through. He uses whoever He chooses, to bless whom He chooses. I am so grateful that one of my brothers would come over when he could, he and his wife. He would always ask if I needed anything. One day he and his wife came over to visit with a bag of groceries. He said, *"Hey sis, we were at Walmart grocery shopping and thought of getting you a bag of groceries too."* It touched my heart so deeply I just hugged him and I tried to hold back my tears.

After they left, I went to my bedroom to thank God my Jehovah Jireh, for He is my provider. I know it was God who put it in my brother's heart to get me some groceries. For if we truly believe and trust God, he always provides. In Matthew 6:26 in the New International Version: "Look at the birds of the air; they do not sow or reap or store away in barns, and yet your heavenly Father feeds them. Are you not much more valuable than they?" My brother was there for me when I needed something to be done in the house. He helped replace the water heater, fixed a leak in the bathroom sink, and the outside faucet. He even helped with a water line leak that I didn't know I had until the water company advised me that my water bill was unusually high compared to previous months. He showed me how to change the oil in the car so that I could save money by doing it myself. I remembered one day him making a remark, "I'll be glad when you find yourself a boyfriend so he can be your handyman." I started laughing. I knew he was joking and it was his way of making light of the situation.

My daughter was getting ready to graduate from high school and she had expressed wanting to continue her education. That meant she would need transportation to get to school and back. I knew my credit situation was not the best, but I stepped out in faith. We both went to look at cars. She spotted a small used, or like they say nowadays a preowned gray pickup truck. I looked at the price to see if it was within the range I could afford. After running my credit, the salesman said he could sell it to me but the interest would be high due to my credit score. After negotiating, I thanked God for walking out of there with the pickup truck. I kept giving God thanks and praise for His goodness in my life and meeting my needs according to his riches in glory (Philippians 4:19 AMP). My daughter had a vehicle to go to school.

My personal life was in shambles. I kept struggling with this spirit of fear. My ex-husband threatened my daughters and my life. He said if he could not be with us the three of us might as well be dead. I knew what he was capable of doing, especially if he was drinking. I had to get a restraining order against him. I was so beat down, broken, and in constant fear. I had lost my sense of identity and my self-esteem. I was literally numb. By the grace of God, I was able to function but it felt like I was operating in auto-mode. This void I felt inside of me was consuming me. The memories of my son were too much to handle. Each time I got home from work his memories would haunt me. I could hear his voice, laughter, and see him running down the hallway. No parent is prepared for a child's death. It does not make a difference whether your child is four or thirty-five, if they die before you. Parents are simply not supposed to outlive their children.

No matter how much I cried in despair to my God Almighty, I still felt so alone in this world. I felt I had hit rock bottom. I did not have the emotional support that I needed. So, I quickly learned to turn to God for comfort, strength and perseverance. Reading scriptures like the one in James 1:2-4 ESV "Count it all joy, my brothers, when you meet trials of various kinds, for you know that the testing of your faith produces steadfastness. And let steadfastness have its full effect, that you may be perfect and complete, lacking in nothing." Those words gave me hope. I was addicted to hearing the word of God. I needed to hear that this too shall pass, words of encouragement and that I was not alone. I needed reassurance that I would be okay. I was just "existing" and every motion or need beyond that seemed nearly impossible. I had to constantly remind myself I still have another child, my daughter who needed me. Listening to Joyce Myers and Bishop T.D. Jakes on television each morning before going to work helped me a lot, and I was reminded God is my rock, my deliverer and strength. I learned to continue to walk in faith and trust the process. Psalms 18:2 in the NIV says "The Lord is my rock, my fortress and my deliverer; my God is my rock, in whom I take refuge, my shield and the horn of my salvation, my stronghold."

The more I relied on my God, read the bible, and stayed in prayer, I began to have dreams that I had no idea what they meant. One night as I was sound asleep, I dreamt of getting out of bed because I heard voices outside in front of the house. I went to the window and saw four men, dressed in white and wearing a black and white hat. Each of them were standing by the doors of the car. The car was a black four-door sedan. I was not able to hear what they were saying. I stood there watching through the window. Finally, all four got into the car and drove off. The next morning, I woke up wondering why in the world did I dream that and what was the meaning. Well, the next night, I was in my bedroom reading when I heard voices outside. I went to the window to see if anybody was there. Lord and behold, I saw exactly what I had dreamt the night before. Up to this day, I'm still baffled.

In another dream I was passing by a village. It looked like a quaint village; the road was covered with cobblestones. As I was walking, I noticed I was stepping on gold coins. I looked down and the road was filled with coins. I bent down to pick the coins up and placed them in a bag I was carrying. No matter how many coins I placed in my bag, the bag never got full. I kept having this dream over and over again for a long time.

Another dream that kept recurring, I would find myself climbing a steep mountain. The higher I climbed, I would get scared because I am afraid of heights. I could literally see my feet as I placed them strategically so that I could hold on as I climbed. Then all of a suddenly I would see male figures dressed in white helping me as I climbed the mountain saying don't be afraid. I always woke up wondering why I kept having that dream.

In another dream, I saw myself floating out in the universe dressed in a white beautiful dress. It looked like a wedding dress. I could see the earth revolving below me. I felt so much peace and full of joy. I could feel a breeze on my face. While I was there floating, I saw a bright light far away. It looked like a golden city. After that, I woke up feeling so at peace. I had no idea of the meaning of the dream, all I know is I felt peace and joy.

The last dream I had that made no sense to me just like the previous ones. I was climbing the mountain again but this time I made it to the top. When I arrived there, I saw twelve men dressed in white robes sitting around a campfire. One of them stood up and said, "There you are. You finally made it. We have been waiting for you. You are one of us now. You will be staying here with us." I answered, "But I need to let my family know where I am." He said, "No." Then I woke up. I had no idea what those recurring dreams meant. All I know is that each time I woke up, I felt so much peace and refreshed. Ready to face the day.

In the meantime, my daughter graduated from junior college and went to the University of Arizona to pursue her degree in Business Administration and Marketing. While still in school, her pickup truck was giving her problems and I knew that eventually I would have to trade it in. The only problem was that the bankruptcy was still showing on my credit. I had been working hard to get my credit score up. As a parent I didn't feel comfortable with her driving the pickup so we swap vehicles. My vehicle was a 1985 Nissan Sentra in mint condition. After two weeks of praying once again I stepped out in faith and asked one of my sisters if she could take me car shopping. We ended up at a Toyota Dealership. I did not go where the preowned vehicles were. I went straight to the new vehicles. I saw a Toyota Corolla. It caught my eye. I looked around and saw the salesman walking towards me. I told him I really like this one. He asked me if I had a trade-in. I said yes but I didn't drive it here, I came with my sister. He said, "Well why don't we go inside, I'll get all the information of the vehicle you are going to trade-in, fill out the paperwork and we'll run your credit." When he said we'll run your credit, I whispered to myself *Lord it's in your hands*. I'm here in faith, trusting in you. Finally, the salesman came into the office and looked at me with bewilderment. He sat down and said, "I have never seen a credit report like this. It shows bankruptcy filed and yet with a high credit score. Did you go to a financial advisor?" I responded, I went to my God. The salesman said the car is yours. Just make sure you bring the pickup truck tomorrow. If I'm not here just park it and leave the keys inside. I leaped in joy! My God, He is a way maker. Where it seems there is no way, he comes through. He reminds us in Isaiah 43:16 ESV "Thus says the Lord, who makes a way in the sea, a path in the mighty waters…" I drove out of the dealership car lot with my first brand new vehicle. All the way home, I kept praising and thanking God!

Chapter 11

Walking in Integrity

Two years later after being promoted to Sergeant, I was promoted to Lieutenant. Once again, God's hand was in the midst. The favor of God was leaning in my direction. The Department of Corrections was going through changes in the Recruitment department. The Director had asked the Wardens to submit a Lieutenant's name from each complex for consideration to be assigned to "special assignment" to the Recruitment department. I was one of the lieutenants chosen.

I was assigned to recruit officers for the Department of Corrections. Once again, working normal hours 8am to 4pm with weekends and holidays off. Some of my peers would ask me how did you land on that cushion position, you just made lieutenant. I knew what they were hinting at but I ignored their remarks. I enjoyed being a recruiter. I met a lot of people who were seeking employment but never thought of applying in Corrections. A lot of them thought they were not cut out to work in such an environment. Those who applied and made it through the hiring process and graduated from C.O.T.A. (Correctional Officers Training Academy) would always make it a point to come and see me in their uniform and thank me for the encouragement and support. During my tenure as a recruiter, I was recognized and received a plague for being the top recruiter that year.

As a lieutenant, I was also appointed as the Complex E.E.O. (Equal Employment Opportunity) Liaison by the Complex Warden. Any employee who felt he or she were being discriminated and treated unfairly on the job because of race, color, religion, sex, national origin, disability, age (40 or older) went to the Warden's office. At the Warden's discretion some were forwarded to me to investigate and report all findings directly to him. This task was very challenging and sensitive because it involved supervisors. At times I had to interview the Deputy Warden of the unit where the employee was assigned. My integrity was at stake. I had to be fair and dig for the truth no matter who was involved. It was an awkward situation because I had to report the truth, not add anything or delete anything. There were times individuals would try to sway me to side in their favor during my interviews but I had to remain neutral and not allow myself to be influenced. I could not compromise my integrity. I had to protect my character and stay true to myself. As a believer in God, I know God expected me to reveal the truth no matter what. Some individuals respected that and some took it in a negative way. They felt I was out to "burn them." I knew I wasn't making any friends but my focus was to please God in everything I did. In Psalm 41:11-12 NIV says "I know that you are pleased with me, for my enemy does not triumph over me. Because of my integrity you uphold me and set me in your presence forever."

This assignment put me in a different light with my peers and co-workers. I don't know if they felt threatened by me or they were just jealous and envious of me because in their eyes I had the Warden's ear. Since I knew how some felt toward me, I had to carry myself in the utmost professional manner; be above reproach. At work, in my office I would refer to Psalms 59:1-2 in the NIV "Deliver me from my enemies, O God; be my fortress against those who are attacking me. Deliver me from evildoers and save me from those who are after my blood." I had to remain prayerful and put on the armor of God daily (Ephesians 6:10-12 NIV). I made it a point to pray each morning before I left the house asking God's protection and to be with me throughout the day. I have learned that we have control how our day will begin and end by commanding our morning with prayer. After one and a half years as a recruiter for the Department, my God put it in my heart to apply for Correctional Captain.

In 2001, I was promoted to Captain and assigned to Eyman Complex, Meadows Unit. Being a captain was very challenging but rewarding. Back then female captains were few in number, especially Hispanic women. During my tenure as Captain, the Department was getting ready to launch an initiative on improving the work life in corrections. A committee was formed representing uniform and non-uniform employees. I was chosen to participate in the committee and work closely with the private consultant the Department had hired to spearhead the initiative. We traveled to all the complexes statewide and spoke randomly to uniformed and non-uniformed employees about the quality of the work life in corrections. Our findings were presented to the Director, the executive team, and all the Wardens. After the presentation, the Director and the executive team worked on which recommendations were doable and made plans to personally travel with his executive team to speak with all the employees. I was honored and humbled to be invited to travel with the Director and the executive team to all the complexes. We flew to each complex. Looking back, I can't help but to think God sure has a sense of humor. I never dreamed I would be traveling with this group of dignitaries. God doesn't use the brightest and the best or the not very influential, he uses the ones people think are nobodies to expose the hollow pretensions of the somebodies (1 Corinthians 1:27 MSG). It opened a door for me to get exposure among all the Administrators, Deputy Wardens and Wardens. My name became well known within the Department. From there I was promoted to Associate Deputy Warden assigned to oversee the operations of one of the private prisons housing Arizona Department of Corrections inmates.

Our day will begin and end by commanding our morning with prayer.

Chapter 12

Letting Go

In 2003, my daughter graduated from the University of Arizona with her Bachelor Degree in Business Administration and Marketing. I was so proud of her! At her graduation, I ran into my ex-husband. I had not seen him since our divorce at the courthouse. It did not surprise me he was there. I knew my daughter was reaching out to him to be part of her life even though we were divorced. I also encouraged her to do so. I never spoke bad about her father to her. I knew that as she got older, she would see just what kind of a man he is without me speaking ill of him. Although, when I saw him, I felt anger toward him. We were cordial to each other that evening for her sake. It was her special day. A day of celebration. She had set a goal to get her degree and she had achieved it with a lot of hard work and determination. I was so proud of her! She didn't stop there. She went on to pursue her Masters in Human Resources.

I went home that evening with a lot of mixed emotions. The next day, I was being convicted. But the anger and resentment I felt toward my ex-husband would not let me. In my mind, I had justifications not to forgive. What happened to me was a traumatic experience of being physically assaulted by the person who was supposed to protect me and supposedly loved me. I was full of anger at him leaving me with all the bills we both had accumulated during our marriage and walking out of our daughter's life with no regard for the emotional damage it did to her. It was bad enough she lost her only brother and then not having her father in her life growing up. I had so much anger and bitterness towards him. I had to make a decision whether to forgive my ex-husband or hold on to the anger, resentment and thoughts of revenge or embrace forgiven and move forward with my life. Deep inside of me I knew I had to forgive for my own sake and forgive myself. One night, as I was reading the Bible, I came across Matthew 6:14 NIV "For if you forgive other people when they sin against you, your heavenly Father will also forgive you" and Romans 12:17-19 NIV "Do not repay anyone evil for evil. Be careful to do what is right in the eyes of everyone...but leave room for God's wrath, for it is written: "It is mine to avenge; I will repay," says the Lord." Then I came to Luke 6:37 in the NIV "Do not judge, and you will not be judged. Do not condemn and you will not be condemned. Forgive, and you will be forgiven." After reading several bible scriptures my conviction grew stronger that I had to forgive my ex-husband, forgive myself, and let go of all bitterness and resentment. I wanted to feel happy again; the only way was to let go of these feelings of bitterness and resentment I felt in my heart and allow the healing process to begin within me.

A few months had passed by when the Lord made a way for me to see my ex-husband again. I happened to visit my daughter at her apartment and unbeknownst to me he was there. I felt nervous. I wasn't expecting to see him. I had to pray a little prayer under my breath. We started making small talk when all of a suddenly I felt the Holy Spirit take over me and I told him that I forgave him for what he did to me. I was releasing to God what my ex-husband did to me. I wanted to put everything behind us and move on with our lives. He also apologized for his actions. He said something that he will always have to live with is what he did to me. After forgiving him, I felt so much peace, even empathy and compassion for him. I don't know why but I did. We parted with a mutual understanding that the important person in our lives is our daughter and if anything, let's be civil with one another for her sake. So I wished him well.

Chapter 13

Overcoming Challenges

In 2006, I was promoted to Deputy Warden at Perryville Complex, Santa Maria Unit. I had made a complete circle in my career. I went back to the unit where I started as a correctional officer. I was told by the Director I was being sent to Santa Maria because it needed attention and from what he had heard from both of his Division Directors I was the person for the job. Of course, I was humbled to hear both Division Directors had such confidence in me. I was told that after a year I would be reassigned closer to home. I was commuting back and forth traveling seventy to seventy-five miles one way. After the year was up, there was talk Deputy Wardens were being moved around, rotated. I was glad to hear that. The driving back and forth was taking its toll. The day came to meet with my Warden and with the Northern Division Director. I walked into the meeting expecting to hear I was being reassigned back to either Eyman or Florence Complexes but that was not the case.

I was told I was needed at Perryville Complex and I was assigned to Lumley Unit instead. The new assignment was considered a promotion and I received a healthy pay increase. The pay increase did not excite me. I was ready to leave Perryville Complex. But when you get to the level of Deputy Warden, you serve at the leisure of the Director. You aren't given a choice on the matter. When I got home, I was so disappointed. When we don't get our way or our expectations are not met, we lose focus on what God has for us. We feel disappointed, sorry for ourselves, and have the tendency of saying God doesn't care. That is when we need to turn to God for direction. In my case, I was wallowing in self-pity; tired of the long drives back and forth.

I was forgetting I had also asked God to help me move to a new location, away from all the memories that kept me suppressed. Ultimately, God will always have his way. Proverbs 19:21 NIV says "Many are the plans in a person's heart, but it is the Lord's purpose that prevails. Because of this, we must submit our plans to God and trust him for direction."

The next morning when I arrived at work, the possibility of moving to Goodyear came to my mind. Doubt immediately consumed my mind, I kept thinking I can't afford a new house. What am I going to do with the one I already have? I certainly can't afford two house payments. I was thinking with my carnal mind, allowing the devil to put doubt instead of what God says in Proverbs 3:5 in the Amplified Bible: "Trust in and rely confidently on the Lord with all your heart and do not rely on your own insight or understanding." The thought of buying a house closer to my job kept haunting me, it would not leave. The Holy Spirit was prompting me to be obedient; to trust in the Lord and rely on him. Matthew 19:26 says Jesus said, "With man this is impossible, but with God all things are possible." I finally stepped out in faith to look for a new house closer to my workplace. I kept reminding myself that everything is possible for those who believe and trust in the Lord

One weekend I went driving through the neighborhoods in the City of Goodyear. I saw a sign saying "Open House." I stopped and went inside the house to look at it. The moment I stepped inside I knew it was not for me. The Realtor Agent looked at me and said, "I can tell this house doesn't interest you." I said not really. I liked open floor plans. She volunteered to help me find something that I would be interested in. See how God works? I never thought of getting a realtor agent and she offered her services without me asking. I told her my financial situation and she said don't worry I am sure we can work something out. She recommended I refinance the house to get the money for the down payment for the new house, and put the house up for rent a month before closing. I followed her instructions. We went to this new housing development not far from where I worked. Looking at the model homes, I fell in love with the open floor plan. We got the paperwork started. I went to the lot where my new house was going to be built. I put my foot on it and prayed over the land for in Joshua 1:3 NIV says "I will give you every place where you set your foot, as I promised Moses."

I refinanced the house, got the money I needed for down payment, and was able to rent the house a month before closing. A copy of the lease was provided to the mortgage company. The whole process went so smoothly with no glitches. I closed on my new house and moved into it with the help of my daughter. I was so happy and thankful to God for my new house. I kept giving thanks and glorifying His name. For God had heard my cries of moving me out of that location and house. It had too many sad and painful memories. No more driving long distances to and from work. I was closer to my workplace. I needed to move to a new location to get a fresh start! By the grace of God, it happened.

Then there was the financial crisis in 2007-2008 and the economy crashed. It cost many people their jobs, their life savings, their homes, or all three. I feel so blessed I made the move before this horrific historical financial meltdown occurred. I was affected by it as well but not as bad as a lot of people were. The tenants renting the house did not renew the lease, he had lost his job. I could not find any tenants to rent the house. I contacted the financial institution whom I had financed it with and told them I could no longer continue to make the house payments. The house went into foreclosure. I was able to continue to make the payments on my new house.

Returning back to Perryville Complex, Santa Maria Unit was very challenging. The culture had changed tremendously, it was totally different from what I remembered. There was no accountability, staff were lax in doing their job, the inmates were not in compliance, and sanitation of the unit was not in acceptable standards. As I set out to explain my expectations to staff, they were told professionalism is a must, in dealing with the inmates. We are not here to punish them but to ensure their safety from other inmates, officer safety and public safety. Abuse of their authority was not going to be tolerated. Policies and procedures will be adhered to. Inmates were told they were to obey orders given from staff and if any inmate felt their rights were being violated, they were to submit a complaint via kite (inmate letter). I would make sure I would look into it. I was out in the yard a lot, making myself visible and available to staff and inmates. I started to see overall improvement. I never had any issues with inmates; staff on the other hand, some not all were not thrilled with accountability.

During my tenure at Santa Maria, I'll never forget this incident that occurred while I was on vacation. It was a bizarre incident, my Warden called me to advise me that one of my ex-officers had committed suicide and a couple of her friend officers were blaming me but not to worry he had it under control. He didn't want me to be blindsided upon returning back to work. This officer had worked for me only three weeks or so, before submitting a transfer to another unit. I did not know much about her. When the Warden told me what happened, I couldn't believe it. I kept wondering what was so devastating that it was the only solution this person thought of. I was aware she lived a perverse lifestyle like many of the female officers assigned to Perryville Complex. That is all I knew of her. Upon returning to work, I found out that my life had been threatened by one of her friend officers. My secretary was surprised to see me and fearful for my life. She said an officer forced herself into my office to do me bodily harm. When the officer saw I was not in the office, she told my secretary that she was going to kill me. Needless to say, this officer was dealt with appropriately.

I was so baffled as to why I was getting blamed for the actions of this officer who committed suicide. I had staff coming to me saying I was not liked by those who lived a perverse lifestyle. I was a threat to them because of my Christianity beliefs. After hearing this, I remember sitting in my office saying the devil is a liar! I rebuke all the lies and demonic attacks coming towards me in Jesus' name. False accusations were being circulated about me throughout the complex. Some staff believed while others didn't. My character and reputation were being attacked. It was not pleasant to know I was being talked about in a derogatory fashion, false rumors being spread throughout the complex, and hateful things said about me.

In spite of all that I had to walk in confidence and boldness. I had to pretend it did not bother me. But it did. I prayed for protection, wisdom, and discernment. If the Lord is with me what can mere mortals do to me (Psalm 118:6-9 NIV). I was also reminded of Isaiah 54:17, "No weapon forged against you will prevail, and you will refute every tongue that accuses you. This is the heritage of the servants of the Lord, and this is their vindication from me," declares the Lord. This particular bible scripture gave me the assurance that I was being protected by the hand of God and not to fear.

When I got promoted to Lumley Unit, again I was told to straighten it out. There were too many cliques, the majority of staff were old-school and set in their ways. I started making changes and holding staff accountable. Some of the officers were glad to see changes for the better were taking place but the group of officers I was warned about were not having it. I was being sabotaged, my name was being dragged in the mud, and I had to defend myself against false accusations. These individuals were not used to being held accountable. They ran the yard how they wanted disregarding systems set in place. It was a very difficult task for me. I knew I was up against the spirit of sabotage, lies, and fear. I was not about to back down and allow this group of officers to defeat me.

Each morning before leaving to work and as I drove to work, I prayed and reminded my God of his word. I was not going to let the devil sabotage me to get me off course with my God. The devil is the master of sabotage. He is a liar and deceiver. He was using this group of officers to rebel against my authority, to lie against me, persecute me, and put fear in me. For God did not give us a spirit of timidity or cowardice or fear, but [He has given us a spirit] of power and of love and of sound judgment and personal discipline [abilities that result in a calm, well-balanced mind and self-control] 2 Timothy 1:7 AMP. I knew I was there for a reason, to change the culture of the unit for the betterment of the inmates housed there and officers who wanted change. I was not going to be defeated in Jesus' name. My trust was in the Lord, He is my refuge and my times are in his hand, and He will rescue me from the hand of my enemies and from my persecutors Psalm 31:15 ESV. The Holy Spirit even put it in my heart to drive around the unit perimeter and pray over the unit and staff. I thank God I never had any issue with the inmates. The inmates started to comply with grooming and housing regulations. The sanitation of the unit was impeccable. My warden was very pleased with the outcome.

I was at Lumley Unit for about a year when I again got promoted. I was promoted to Deputy Warden of Operations at Lewis Complex. I was assigned there for about eight months then reassigned to Phoenix Complex. Each time I was promoted, I was getting a pay increase. God was smiling on me. In James

1:12 GNB “Happy are those who remain faithful under trials, because when they succeed in passing such a test, they will receive as their reward the life which God has promised to those who love him.” It felt great not having to count pennies to buy groceries or being able to buy shoes, or a blouse without having to worry about not having enough. All my bills were paid ahead of time. No more bill collectors harassing me! I was beginning to see the blessings manifest in my life. God is looking for people whose heart is fully His and are loyal and faithful to Him. If we are faithful to God, He will show himself strong toward us in all we do. When we are faithful, we will be rich, well supplied for He is our Provider. Proverbs 28:20 KJV says “A faithful man shall abound with blessings...”

When we don't get our way
or our expectations are not met,
we lose focus on what God has for us.

Chapter 14

God is good

I was being blessed in so many ways that I wanted to be a blessing to someone else. Some of my siblings were planning to go to Hawaii and I was invited. I had never been to Hawaii. We had our first vacation planning meeting. We started making plans, figuring out the cost, and what the itinerary was going to be. One of my brothers said that he was not going because it was too expensive. When he said that, my heart broke but I didn't say anything. It reminded me of when I couldn't afford food on the table so I understood where he was coming from

The time was nearing for our Hawaii vacation. I had the trip paid for but little did anybody know the vacation trip was not for me but for my brother and his wife. I thought there will be plenty of time for me to go to Hawaii. Yes, the brother who said he could not afford it; the brother who was always there for me when I was struggling financially, that brother. I wanted to surprise him and his wife; it was my way of showing my gratitude for being there for me in time of need.

I will never forget my brother's reaction when I placed the plane tickets in his hands and told him that he and his wife were going to Hawaii. Up until that moment, I had never experienced such a joy of giving before! I understood why it says in the bible, "It is more blessed to give than to receive" (Acts 20:35). I will never forget that unforgettable moment! Today, my husband and I, along with my daughter, go to Hawaii every year!

In the year 2007, I purchased my first Mercedes Benz! I was floating in the air. I never dreamed I would be driving a Mercedes Benz. God's favor was on my life. I give God all the glory. He made it possible! However, the devil tried to keep me from enjoying my new car by making me feel undeserving, not worthy, and embarrassed. It's funny how the devil tries to keep you in bondage. The feeling of unworthiness makes you feel insufficient in worth, undeserving; lack value or merit; worthless or unsuitable, befitting. The devil is a liar! He does not stand in the truth because there is no truth in him. When he lies, he speaks what is natural to him, for he is a liar and the father of lies and half-truths (John 8:44 AMP). We need to remind ourselves that God wants us to have an abundant life. John 10:10 AMP says "The thief comes only in order to steal and kill and destroy. I came that they may have life, and have it in abundance [to the full, till it overflows]".

God did not forget that time when out of desperation I told my daughter one of these days, we will have a NICE car! At that time, I was driving a Geo Metro, it had the horsepower of a lawnmower. I used to get teased by my siblings. One Fourth of July, we were visiting one of my sisters in California. On the way back, we agreed to caravan back home but everybody was passing us, leaving us behind. My Geo could only go so fast. I never heard the end of that from my siblings.

In 2009, I decided it was time to retire from Corrections. However, in 2012, I returned to Corrections and worked in a private prison operated by GEO Group, Inc. I returned back as a favor to one of my colleagues. After two years of working there, I fully retired. Some people ask how do you know you are ready to retire. From my perspective, your passion for what you are doing runs out. You no longer have that will or desire to continue doing what once used to be self-rewarding and exciting. In my case I felt my God given assignment had ended.

I am still in AWE how God from the very beginning was with me throughout my life and kept me even though it appeared at times He was far away. Now I understand that our existence here on earth is to have an intimate relationship with him, remain faithful, trust, and believe in him. We have to walk by faith because “without faith it is impossible to please God, because anyone who comes to him must believe that he exists and that he rewards those who earnestly seek him” (Hebrews 11:6 NIV).

We all go through a valley of darkness; our lives seem gloomy and hopeless. Those are the times we experience sorrows, hurt, rejection, loss of a loved one, divorce, sickness, physical abuse or assault, financial struggles, or character assassinations. God never said we would not face trials and tribulations. He will however help us as we go through the process if we believe in him. In John 16:33 ESV “I have said these things to you, that in me you may have peace. In the world you will have tribulation, but take heart; I have overcome the world.”

As we go through the process, we must keep the faith and trust in the Lord. He has a plan for us. Jeremiah, verse 29:11 NIV “For I know the plans I have for you,” declares the Lord, “plans to prosper you and not to harm you, plans to give you hope and a future.” He already has a plan for us! My reliance and total dependence on God through my sufferings and struggles is what has brought me through. I had to stay plugged-in to the Source – God. God never said he would take away our trials and tribulations but to count it all joy, when we meet trials of various kinds. Through the testing of our faith, through experience produces endurance leading to spiritual maturity, and inner peace (James 1:2-3 AMP). God wants us to have faith in him and to be obedient. To believe that what we pray for will come to pass if it's according to His will. Don’t let doubt take over. James 1:6 NIV says, “But when you ask, you must believe and not doubt, because the one who doubts is like a wave of the sea, blown and tossed by the wind." I am thankful and give God all the glory for He has healed me, given me restoration and wholeness in my life. He has richly blessed me in every area of my life. There is peace in me, the peace that surpasses all understanding. The kind of peace only He can give.

I pray that after reading this book, my testimony of how God brought me through during the lowest points in my life will bless you, encourage you, and bring you into the fullness of what God has for you, so that you may walk in your anointing in your life. Trust the process. God is a Way Maker, Miracle Worker, Promise Keeper, and Light in the Darkness.

Remember we are more than conquerors...WE ARE OVERCOMERS.

God never said we would
not face trials and tribulations.
He will, however, help us as we go
through the process, if we believe in him.

Endorsements

Pastor Patricia Kimani-Muiruri:

"At a time when not only the world is experiencing a shift in the landscape of life due to global crises, there is also the issue of the family unit under several attacks. Maria Drake has provided a much-needed relief through her new book *"Overcomer"*, drawing strength from her own experiences dealing with life tragedies and yet finding hope in her faith to not only survive, but thrive. I highly recommend this book and I also congratulate my sister-in-Christ. I pray that this truth will reach millions of souls across the globe. Amen!"

Bishop Eric O. Minta:

There is an African Proverb that goes " If you educate a woman, you educate a nation." I have always admired the uniqueness of women and I know for certain that Maria Drake's testimony will empower many women. I highly recommend this book "Overcome"

Minister Veda Platt:

Maria Drake is an anointed woman of God, with a heart for women, especially those who are new to the faith. This book, *"Overcomer"*, is perfect for not only the new but also the seasoned in Christ.

Biography

Maria is a retired Deputy Warden of Operations, Author of *"Overcomer: A Memoir"*, mother, and wife. She has a degree in Administration of Criminal Justice from Central Arizona College.

Maria enjoys helping people reach their fullest potential. She mentored and helped develop employees for possible promotion and/or provided avenues for self-improvement to assist in their growth within the organization. Her passion is to inspire, encourage and empower women of all ages – and instill that with God all is possible if you have faith and believe regardless of circumstances.

Married with two children, she and her husband love to travel and are very committed in their faith in God.

Made in the USA
Middletown, DE
18 April 2022

64177652R00053